You and Your Lodger

Cavendish
Publishing
Limited

London • Sydney • Portland, Oregon

This book is supported by a Companion Website, created to keep titles in the *Pocket Lawyer* series up to date and to provide enhanced resources for readers.

Key features include:

◆ forms and letters, in a ready-to-use Word format
   Access all the material you need at the click of a button

◆ updates on key developments
   Your book won't become out of date

◆ links to useful websites
   No more fruitless internet searches

www.cavendishpublishing.com/pocketlawyer

You and Your Lodger

Rosy Border

Cavendish
Publishing
Limited

London • Sydney • Portland, Oregon

Second edition first published in Great Britain 2004 by
Cavendish Publishing Limited, The Glass House,
Wharton Street, London WC1X 9PX, United Kingdom
Telephone: + 44 (0)20 7278 8000   Facsimile: + 44 (0)20 7278 8080
Email: info@cavendishpublishing.com
Website: www.cavendishpublishing.com

Published in the United States by Cavendish Publishing
c/o International Specialized Book Services,
5824 NE Hassalo Street, Portland,
Oregon 97213-3644, USA

Published in Australia by Cavendish Publishing (Australia) Pty Ltd
45 Beach Street, Coogee, NSW 2034, Australia
Email: info@cavendishpublishing.com.au
Website: www.cavendishpublishing.com.au

© Border, Rosy   2004

The first edition of this title was previously published by The Stationery Office

British Library Cataloguing in Publication Data
Border, Rosy –
You and your lodger – 2nd ed – (Pocket lawyer)
1 Landlord and tenant – Great Britain 2 Lodging-houses –
Law and legislation – Great Britain
I Title
346.4'10434

Library of Congress Cataloguing in Publication Data
Data available

ISBN 1-85941-860-0

1 3 5 7 9 10 8 6 4 2

Printed and bound in Great Britain

Contents

Disclaimer

This book puts *you* in control. This is an excellent thing, but it also makes *you* responsible for using it properly. Few washing machine manufacturers will honour their guarantee if you don't follow their 'instructions for use'. In the same way, we are unable to accept liability for any loss arising from mistakes or misunderstandings on your part. So take time to read this book carefully.

Although this book points you in the right direction, reading one small book will not make you an expert, and there are times when you may need to take advice from professionals. This book is not a definitive statement of the law, although we believe it to be accurate as at September 2003.

The authors and publisher cannot accept liability for any advice or material that becomes obsolete due to subsequent changes in the law after publication, although every effort will be made to show any changes in the law that take place after the publication date on the companion website.

About the author

Rosy Border, author of this title and series editor of the *Pocket Lawyer* series, has a first class honours degree in French and has worked in publishing, lecturing, journalism and the law. A prolific author and adapter, she stopped counting after 150 titles. She owns and manages several properties, which she describes as her 'pension fund'. Rosy and her husband, John Rabson, live in rural Suffolk and have a grown up family. Rosy enjoys DIY, entertaining and retail therapy in French markets.

Acknowledgments

Grateful thanks to Mark Fairweather, solicitor, whose brain child the Lodger Agreement was, and to John Rabson, Chartered Engineer, for IT support and coffee.

Welcome

Welcome to *Pocket Lawyer*. Let's face it, the law is a maze and you are likely to get lost unless you have a map. This book is your map through the part of the maze that deals with taking in a lodger.

We put *you* in control

This book empowers you. This is a good thing, but being in control means responsibility as well as power, so please use this book properly. Read it with care and don't be afraid to make notes – I have left wide margins for you to do just that. Take your time – do not skip anything:

o   everything is there for a purpose;

o   if anything were unimportant, I would have left it out.

Think of yourself as a driver using a road map. The map tells you the route, but it is up to you to drive carefully along it.

Sometimes you are in danger of getting out of your depth and you will need to take professional advice. Watch out for the hazard sign.

Sometimes I stop to empower you to do something. Look out for the 'Power points' sign.

Clear English rules OK

Client to solicitor who has just drafted a contract for him: 'This *can't* be legal – I can understand it!'

Our style is WYSIWYG – what you see is what you get.

Some legal documents have traditionally been written in archaic language, often known as 'law-speak'. This term also extends to the practice of using the names of legal cases as shorthand for legal concepts. This wording has stood the test of time – often several centuries – and has been hallowed by the courts. Some of the words used sound just like everyday language, but beware – it is a kind of specialist shorthand. When I *do* need to use technical language, I offer clear explanations (see 'Buzzwords', p xiii). These words appear in the text in **bold** so you can check their meaning.

A note on gender

This book is unisex. I acknowledge that there are both male and female members of every group and I try to allow for that in the text by using, wherever possible, the generic *they/them* rather than *he/she*, *him/her*, etc.

Click onto the website

www.cavendishpublishing.com/pocketlawyer

Getting the most from this book

Why write an agreement in a foreign language in preference to plain English? What is important is that your agreement with your lodger is expressed in clear, unambiguous language that accurately reflects your intentions and which both of you understand. The Lodger Agreement in this book is a WYSIWYG document.

If you follow my advice you should end up with a Lodger Agreement that:

o   does what you want it to do;

o   is fair to both you and your lodger;

o   is legally sound;

o   you as a non-lawyer can understand.

It is crucial not to lose sight of the legal side. Both you
and your lodger will have duties and responsibilities
and it is important to spell those out at the very
beginning. This book sets out these duties and
responsibilities and embodies them in an agreement that
is fair to both you and your lodger. It also alerts you to
the possible problems and pitfalls on the way. It:

o   provides the general information that professional
    advisers would give you on the subject, if only they
    had the time to do so, and if only you had the
    money to pay them;

o   tells you many things that experienced landlords
    took years to find out the hard way;

o   shows you the terms, or 'buzzwords', that are
    important, and explains what they mean;

o   answers some of the most frequently asked
    questions on the subject;

o   advises you on choosing a lodger;

o   provides a plain English 'Lodger Agreement' to
    meet most needs, together with all the additional
    paperwork that you are likely to need;

o   helps you to keep good records of your transactions
    with your lodger;

o   is supported by a regularly updated companion
    website.

Buzzwords

Here are some terms you will come across in this book. In this section I make their meanings clear. The terms appear in **bold** in the text.

breach – the breaking or ignoring of a rule or agreement (as 'breach of or non-compliance with the Lodger's obligations under this Agreement' in the Standard Provisions (see p 51)). Lawyers faced with someone who has broken the rules say that that person is 'in breach'.

deposit – sometimes called a *damage deposit*: a sum of money (typically the equivalent of one month's rent) which the lodger hands to the landlord at the beginning of their stay as a kind of guarantee of good behaviour. At the end of the lodger's stay, the landlord returns the deposit in full if all is well, or uses all or part of it to cover any unpaid rent, cleaning, damage, etc (see Chapter 5).

deposit guarantee scheme – a way of enabling landlords to take in lodgers who cannot afford a **deposit**. Typically, a local authority or housing charity gives the landlord a guarantee or bond to cover a maximum of one month's rent, but no money changes hands unless the lodger misbehaves in some way, when the local authority pays the landlord and claims the money back from the ex-lodger (see p 44 for a full explanation).

HMO – a house in multiple occupation: typically a large house split into several separate flats or bedsits (see p 13).

housing benefit – help towards the rent of a person on state benefits (see Chapter 4).

inventory – a list of fittings, furnishings and equipment in the premises, the lodger occupies (see the sample inventory, p 55).

landlord – the person to whom the rent is paid. The word is unisex – there are lots of female landlords.

licensee – a tenant has a tenancy but, broadly speaking, a lodger has a 'licence to occupy' and is sometimes referred to as a 'licensee'. I have included this term here because, although I do not use it in this book, you may come across it if you surf the internet for more information about, for example, lodgers' rights.

lodger – someone who lives with you in your own home, or in a part of the same building as you, in return for rent (see 'Are you a resident landlord?', p 1).

Rent-a-Room scheme – a tax concession granted by the Inland Revenue to encourage people to rent out spare rooms in their homes (see 'A present from the taxman', p 62, for a description of how the scheme works).

resident landlord – the householder in a property where a lodger lives in return for rent. You are not a resident landlord unless the two of you live under the same roof (see 'Are you a resident landlord?', p 1).

serve – law-speak for sending or handing over a legal document, as in to 'serve a notice to quit'.

statutory – laid down by law (statute) and therefore obligatory.

Frequently asked questions (FAQs)

When I was in lodgings as a student there was no written agreement and everything went just fine. Why are you so insistent on formal contracts?

How do you know that your **landlord** did not have a formal contract with your university accommodation office? Chances are they did! Contracts are important because:

o they lay down the ground rules from the start;

o they protect both you and your **lodger** if anything goes wrong;

o some people may need reminding about what they promised to do and not to do.

I am receiving income support. Would taking in a lodger affect my benefits?

Almost certainly. Your income from your lodger – *which it is a criminal offence not to declare* – will be taken into account when your benefits entitlement is assessed. It might still be worth your while, however (see 'Are you allowed to take in lodgers?', p 2).

I am taking in a lodger who will pay a monthly rent. Do I need to provide a rent book?

No, you don't. Rent books are obligatory only if the rent is payable *weekly*. You are, of course, free to provide a rent book if you wish (see suggestions on p 61). You will still have to keep good records of payments. Give your lodger a receipt for each month's rent (you will find a sample receipt in 'Notices and letters' (p 70) and on the companion website) and keep copies on file.

Can I charge whatever rent I like?

For a **lodger** who is not receiving state benefits, the answer is yes. In practice, of course, you are unlikely to command more than the going rate for your district and the type of accommodation. Rent is a matter to be agreed between you and your lodger; if you find someone willing to pay over the odds, good luck to you. However, there might be tax to pay if your gross income from rent exceeds £4,250 in the tax year (see 'A present from the taxman', p 62).

If you take in a lodger who is receiving state benefits, the local authority, who has its own guidelines to follow, may not pay as much as a private lodger would. In theory, you could charge the going rate and ask the lodger to make up the shortfall, but how likely would you be to get your money? (See Chapter 4.)

Can I charge whatever deposit I like?

Deposits are another matter to be decided between you and your lodger, but in general one or two months' rent would be reasonable (see Chapter 5).

I am thinking of taking in two young ladies in a twin-bedded room. Am I allowed to do this, or does each lodger have to have their own room?

The answers are yes and no, respectively. Sharing is a matter for you to agree with your lodgers, who would obviously want some say in the choice of room-mates. If they are happy sharing a room, that's fine.

A young unmarried couple would like my double room. Am I allowed to take them in as lodgers?

The law is silent on this matter, and it is entirely up to you to decide whether or not you want this couple in your home. How stable does their relationship seem? If they part company, you may be put in an uncomfortable position – can the remaining lodger afford to pay the whole rent, or will you have to ask them to leave too? However, this is a human relations problem, not a legal one.

Does my lodger's accommodation have to have its own lock and key?

The law is silent on this subject. This is something for you and your **lodger** to decide between you. Personally, if I gave my lodger a lockable room I would keep a spare key, which I would *never* use unless they lost theirs (which has been known!), or in the case of an emergency.

What rights of access do I have to my lodger's accommodation?

The sample Lodger Agreement (p 50) gives you unlimited access at 'reasonable times'. Unless you have arranged access for cleaning, bedmaking, etc, you will, of course, respect your lodger's privacy and ask their permission to enter their quarters, but you need to be able to get in to carry out your responsibilities (electrical/gas safety checks, for example), and in an emergency, when, of course, you can go in without asking permission.

Will I have to pay tax on the income from my lodger?

Not unless your gross income from your lodger is more than £4,250 in a given tax year (which runs from 6 April of one year to 5 April of the next) (see 'A present from the taxman', p 62, for details).

£4,250 tax free sounds wonderful. Does this mean £4,250 for each lodger?

No. Sorry. If you take in two lodgers the £4,250 is shared between them.

Who is responsible for cleaning my lodger's room?

This is something to be agreed between you and your lodger. A common arrangement is for the **landlord** to see to the cleaning of shared areas such as the kitchen, bathroom, landing, etc, while the lodger keeps their own room clean and tidy – in which case, show them where you keep the vacuum cleaner or even provide them with one of their very own!

Have I any control over my lodger's visitors and how long they stay?

Yes, indeed. This is a matter for you to agree with your lodger at the beginning. It's your home and you can set the house rules. The sample Lodger Agreement (p 50) makes no restrictions but makes your **lodger** responsible for any nuisance or damage caused by their visitors.

How much notice do I have to give my lodger if I want them to leave?

If you share essential accommodation (such as a bathroom, lavatory or kitchen) with your lodger, there is no legal minimum period. Otherwise, the legal minimum is four weeks. In practice you should give four weeks to be both safe and friendly, and the Lodger Agreement (p 50) reflects this (see also Chapter 8).

Someone once told me that unless I provided food my lodger would be classed as a tenant and I wouldn't be able to evict them without taking them to court. Is this true?

I've heard these tales too: the slice of bread put outside the lodger's door and so on. The food question does not apply if you are a **resident landlord** (see 'Are you a resident landlord?', p 1).

If I died while my lodger was in residence, could the lodger claim the right to stay on?

Such things have been known. Have no fear, however; the sample Lodger Agreement (p 50) enables whoever takes over from you to step into your shoes as **landlord** and enforce the agreement in your place.

I am thinking of making some alterations to my house to provide extra facilities for my two lodgers. Do I need planning permission for this?

The answer is a definite maybe. It is a matter of scale; if you do something requiring planning permission, or if you stray into **HMO** territory, you may have to satisfy certain **statutory** requirements (see 'Adapting your home – the rules', p 11, and if in doubt, call your local authority for advice).

Is there any insurance I can take out against rent arrears?

Yes, there is and it may or may not be worth your while to take it out. Call your local insurance broker, or check out one of the numerous insurance websites (see also 'Are you insured?', p 15).

If my lodger has a TV in their room, will they need a licence?

Your own TV licence covers all the sets in your home and, in general, a **lodger** will be sharing your home. Of course, if you yourself have no TV and your lodger brings one in, a licence will be needed and it is up to you and your lodger to agree who should pay for it.

I live alone and receive a 25% reduction in my council tax on account of this. Will taking in a lodger mean I have to pay more council tax?

There is no short answer to this because some lodgers, such as students, would not attract council tax. Also, a lodger who pays council tax elsewhere (as might be the case with someone working away from home) gets special treatment. Call the council tax department of your local authority.

What happens if a lodger harasses me or a member of my family?

It depends how serious the incident is. Physical violence, racial and sexual abuse are, of course, police matters. Most local authority housing departments can advise landlords: call your local council and ask. Meanwhile, you don't have to put up with harassment in your own home. **Serve** your lodger with a 'Notice to Quit', an example of which you will find in 'Notices and letters' at the back of the book.

Before you start

Read this chapter carefully before you take in a **lodger**, or even before you start looking for one.

Are you a resident landlord?

The distinguishing feature of a lodger is that they live under the same roof as their **landlord**, who is often known as a **resident landlord**. A plain English definition of a lodger is 'someone who lives with a landlord in the landlord's own home, or in a part of the same building, in return for a weekly or monthly rent'.

The law differentiates between a *lodger* (who has a resident landlord) and a *tenant* (who hasn't). You need to be sure whether you are dealing with a lodger or a tenant, because the law gives much more protection to tenants than it gives to lodgers. For example, it is much easier for a landlord to get a lodger to leave than to evict a tenant (see Chapter 8).

A legalistic definition of a *tenant* is 'a person who is granted exclusive possession of a property for a fixed or ascertainable period of time, in return for a weekly or monthly rent'. There are two key elements here: *'exclusive possession'* – which means the tenant does not share any part of the premises with the landlord, and *'ascertainable period of time'* – which means the tenancy agreement has to say *when* the tenancy is to start and *when* (or *how*, such as 'two months' notice') it is to end. During that 'ascertainable period of time', a tenant enjoys exclusive use of the property, as opposed to a lodger, who does not.

It is common for lodgers to have a room of their own but to share other rooms, such as the landlord's bathroom, lavatory, kitchen, etc. Some lodgers receive services from the landlord – cleaning, laundry, meals and so on – as part of the deal. Many do not, however, and the absence of meals or services (see 'FAQs', p xviii) does not stop someone from being a lodger.

People renting self-contained accommodation, such as a bedsit, can still be lodgers as long as:

o the landlord lives in the same building;

o the building is the landlord's only or main home and is not, for example, a purpose-built block of flats with the landlord occupying one flat and the lodger/tenant another.

By now, you will probably be sure in your own mind whether or not you are a resident landlord. If you are still unsure, however, you will find an exhaustive (and I fear sometimes exhausting) examination of the subject in *Letting Rooms in Your Home, A Guide for Resident Landlords*, from the Office of the Deputy Prime Minister (ODPM), 17 January 2003, available from Citizens Advice Bureaux (CABs) and on the internet at www.housing.odpm.gov.uk (see 'Useful contacts' for details, p 75).

If you are a resident landlord, read on. If you are not a resident landlord, you probably need *Letting Your Property* in this series.

Are you allowed to take in lodgers?

Before you read any further, you need to be sure that you have the right to take in a **lodger**.

You are receiving state benefits

If you are receiving state benefits – whether you own your home or rent it – your income from your lodger, *which it is a criminal offence not to declare*, will be taken into account when your benefits entitlement is assessed.

Do not give up hope, however. You could still come out on top, and in some districts where there is a severe accommodation shortage, people claiming state benefits are actively encouraged to find out whether they would still gain from taking in a lodger. In Essex, for example, the Harlow Accommodation Project advertises free advice and help with deposit guarantees, and many other local authorities run similar initiatives. Wherever you live, the amount you are allowed to keep is the same. Now read on.

Here is an example based on figures from the website of a local authority in Essex:

Are you providing any meals?

o   No – you are allowed to keep the first £4 of rent per week. If you don't include meals but do include *heating*, you are (at the time of writing) allowed to keep the first £4 per week of rent (see above) plus an extra £9.40. The rest of the rent is taken into account as income and a deduction is taken from your benefit.

o   Yes – you are allowed to keep the first £20 per week of rent and only 50% of the remainder counts as income. So, if the rent is £80 per week, you are allowed to keep £50.

There is a disadvantage in including meals and/or heating in the deal if your lodger is also receiving state benefits. In this case, their own benefit may be cut if their rent includes meals and/or heating. It can get quite complicated and the sensible thing to do is to call your local CAB or housing aid centre to see how taking in a lodger would affect *your* benefits (see also Chapter 4).

You are an owner-occupier

o   If you are an owner-occupier, and you own your home outright (that is, without a mortgage), the answer is generally yes (but see 'Your property is leasehold', p 4).

o   If you are an owner-occupier, and there is a mortgage on your home, the government booklet *Letting Rooms in Your Home* (see 'Useful contacts', p 75) advises you to ask your mortgage lender's permission before taking in a lodger. The Landlordzone website (www.landlordzone.co.uk)

advises this too. (Incidentally, Landlordzone also recommends this book!)

Additionally, by way of research, I called three building societies who said they would always say 'yes', but appreciated being asked. I would add that when you do ask your mortgage lender, you should make it clear that you are *taking in a lodger*, not *creating a tenancy*. Emphasise that:

o you are continuing to live in your home; *and*

o you will be sharing accommodation with your lodger.

Moving out of your home and renting it out is a different matter entirely. Your mortgage lender would not only insist on your asking permission, but charge you a fee for this!

Your property is leasehold

If your home is leasehold (most flats are leasehold), whether it is mortgaged or not, you must check the terms of your lease.

If your lease says you need the permission of the person or organisation that owns the freehold of the building (often called the 'ground rent **landlord**') to sub-let (most do), you *must* get that permission before taking anyone into your home. If you do not do so, you will be contravening the terms of your lease, which is a serious matter, and in a worst-case scenario you could lose your home.

You are a secure council tenant

If you are a secure council tenant, as opposed, for example, to a council tenant in temporary accommodation, you have the right to take in a lodger. This is explained clearly in a booklet from the ODPM, called *Your Rights as a Council Tenant – The Council Tenants' Charter* (see 'Useful contacts', p 75), or from your local CAB. Many councils issue their own leaflets, based on the ODPM material, and run their own websites. There are some splendid websites with extremely clear explanations. Your own council may offer one of these. Try keying in the name of your local authority and the words 'lodger advice' or 'letting rooms' and see what you get.

You are a housing association tenant

If you are a tenant of a housing association, the answer is probably yes, but rules may differ and you should check with your own housing association before taking in a lodger. As above, your housing association is likely to issue leaflets and/or provide a website about this. In researching this book I came across some admirable websites; your housing association may provide one of these.

You are a private tenant

If you are a tenant in privately rented accommodation, the answer depends on the terms of your tenancy agreement – and in many cases on your landlord's goodwill. Check your tenancy agreement and talk to your landlord if you are not sure. Your landlord may well ask for reassurance about insurance (see p 15) before agreeing.

Are you happy about sharing?

Whatever your motives for taking in a **lodger**, you must realise that having other people living in your home and sharing facilities is a rather intimate thing. There is a subtle alteration in the atmosphere. It is going too far to say 'your home's no longer your own', but you are no longer alone in your home. Someone will walk on your carpets, use your lavatory, possibly cook on your stove. Will this bother you?

Some people who have lived alone for a while find it very hard to contemplate taking in even the quietest and most considerate of lodgers. People like this would rather be short of money than share their home. There would be someone else living under their roof and invading their personal space and, however harmonious their relationship with the other person, they would feel uncomfortable about it. If this thought really worries you, consider taking on a paper round before you take in a lodger!

Consider your motives

There are many possible reasons for taking a **lodger** into your home. Why are *you* contemplating this step? Here are four obvious reasons. I expect you will be able to think of others.

○ **Financial necessity**

Many people take in lodgers to make ends meet. They have a spare room and the lodger's rent helps with the rent or mortgage, the heating and other household bills. Realistically speaking, these **landlords** probably cannot afford *not* to share their home.

○ **Child care/pet care**

I have met landlords whose lodgers do a weekly evening of baby-sitting as part of the deal. The Gingerbread website (www.gingerbread.org.uk: see 'Useful contacts', p 76) advocates this too. Pet care could be another consideration. Students who miss their own pets will often enjoy helping to look after yours. Before handing over your children or pets you will, of course, vet your lodger very thoroughly indeed.

○ **Space to spare**

Other people – empty-nesters, perhaps – find the family home has become too large for their current needs. It seems a pity to let all that space go to waste, and the money would come in handy.

○ **Companionship**

Some people are just lonely. I have come across several very pleasant people who have taken in a lodger for 'the sound of a key in the lock and a friendly voice in the hall'.

2

Preparing for your lodger: your duties and responsibilities

Let's start with one important question.

Is your property habitable?

Anyone whose job entails visiting people in their homes will tell you that different people have different ideas of what is and is not habitable. You and your family may be living quite happily in a property which is gently crumbling around you and has rising damp, mould, penetrating damp, dry rot, wet rot, rats and cockroaches, flammable furniture, dangerous gas appliances and dodgy electrical wiring. It's your home and, within reason, how you keep it is your affair: 'an Englishman's home is his castle' after all.

The law is unlikely to take much interest in your home unless it catches fire or someone actually complains to the public health department that it is a health hazard to the rest of the neighbourhood. However, as soon as you invite a lodger into your home, the law – theoretically at least – swings into action to protect them from harm.

This is because someone other than you or your family has come to live in your home. This someone is your **lodger**, who has rights. From an ordinary householder you are suddenly transformed into a **landlord**. As a landlord, you have a **statutory** duty – a duty which you cannot dodge, even if your lodger is on your side – to provide your lodger with accommodation that meets all the legal requirements. Can you tick all the boxes in this checklist?

Is your home:

o   Safe, especially from fire risks? [   ]

o   Fit to live in? [   ]

o   Free from serious disrepair? [   ]

In more detail, this means:

o   The property must be weatherproof and free from damp. [   ]

o   It must be free from vermin and insect infestation. [   ]

o   The electrical wiring must be safe. [   ]

o   Any gas appliances must be safe. [   ]

o   There must be access to a wash basin, bath (or shower) and lavatory. [   ]

o   There must be adequate heating, lighting and ventilation. [   ]

o   Flats and bedsits must have adequate means of escape in case of fire. [   ]

o   Furniture, such as sofas, in the accommodation the lodger uses must be flame-retardant. [   ]

If you find this list daunting, you need to ask yourself whether – quite apart from your statutory duties – any lodger is going to pay good money to live in accommodation that is dirty, badly equipped, cold or even dangerous! In any case, help is available (see 'Power points', below).

Who can help?

o   If you are not sure whether your home is electrically safe, you can arrange a free electrical safety check. Contact your own electricity supplier in the first instance (there should be a display advertisement in your local telephone directory). They should be able to give you a freephone number to call.

○ Poorly maintained gas appliances cause many deaths every year. If you use gas in your home, you should, for your own peace of mind, get your appliances checked regularly for safety. If you take in a **lodger**, you have a **statutory** duty under the Gas Safety (Installation and Use) Regulations 1998 to get your gas appliances checked for safety every year. You must use a proper CORGI (Council of Registered Gas Installers) registered fitter, who will issue you with two copies of a landlord's gas safety certificate – one copy for you and one for your lodger (to find a CORGI fitter near you, see 'Useful contacts', p 75).

Note that if you have a lodger, *all* gas installations in your home – not just in the parts of your home which are occupied by your lodger – must be checked for safety every year. Once you have the safety certificate, *make a note in your diary to remind you to renew it before it expires.* Unlike the DVLA, nobody will remind you that your old licence is about to expire.

○ If your home is seriously substandard in some way, you might qualify for a grant, regardless of whether you take in a lodger or not. There are grants available to provide essential facilities, such as bathrooms, for homes which have none. There are also government initiatives to help make homes more energy efficient, and a great deal of public money is available. Provision of grants, and the way schemes are administered, varies from region to region. Call your local Citizens Advice Bureau (CAB) and ask what is available in your area.

○ Call in your local fire prevention officer (FPO) to check your home for fire risks. This is a free service and it is worth making friends with your local FPO, even if you do not take in a lodger (see 'Power point', p 15, for details).

○ A lot of furniture is padded with foam, which is comfortable to sit on but can be lethal if it catches fire. You have probably read terrifying tales of foam furniture either bursting into flames or giving off poisonous smoke. The same foam is perfectly safe if it is treated to make it flame-retardant. After several tragedies, laws were passed to outlaw untreated foam furniture, and now all new items *must* have been treated. The law does nothing to prevent you from filling your own home with dangerous furnishings, but it does protect lodgers and tenants. The Furniture (Fire Safety) Regulations 1993 require all sofas, chairs, mattresses and other soft furnishings in rental accommodation (which includes anywhere occupied by your lodger) to be flame-retardant unless they were made before 1950. For more detailed information, call your local trading standards department.

We all like a bargain, but if you are considering buying some second-hand furniture for your **lodger's** room you will be breaking the law unless the furniture you buy is flame retardant. Turn the item upside down and look for the label. A typical label – this one came from a sofa – will say something along the lines of:

> ### 'CARELESSNESS CAUSES FIRE'
>
> This item does not require Section 3 interliner. All foams, fillings and composites have been tested by our suppliers to ensure compliance with the relevant ignitability test. Covers and fillings are cigarette resistant. Covers are match resistant. Further details are available from your retailer.

Don't buy unless there is a label. The regulations have been around for a long time and there should be plenty of safe items around.

○   For vermin or insect infestation, contact your local authority. Some charge for their services, but many don't. There is no need to feel embarrassed; I know of a flea invasion – bitten ankles, no less – caused by a stray cat that a kindly family adopted. The same cat brought home several live mice, which escaped and set up home behind a skirting board. The pest control man said that both problems were very common and did not indicate that the householder was dirty or negligent!

If you let 'unfit' property – property which does not meet all the **statutory** requirements listed above – you can get into serious trouble. If the worst happens and someone dies or is injured through your negligence or carelessness, you can be sued!

Now keep it like that!

Having provided accommodation which meets the **statutory** requirements, you must keep it that way throughout your lodger's stay (unless, of course, the damage is caused by the **lodger**).

Adapting your home – the rules

You might want to adapt or alter your home in some way to make your **lodger** more comfortable: adding a shower, perhaps, or dividing one very large room into a bedroom and a sitting room or study area. Who do you need to ask?

o   If you rent your home from a council, a housing association or a private **landlord**, you will certainly need to get their permission first.

o   If your home is leasehold, check your lease. You may need your ground rent landlord's permission.

o   If you are an owner-occupier with a mortgage, you may need your mortgage lender's permission. They would want to know of any alteration that might affect the value or stability of the property.

o   In some situations, you may need to check with your insurer. Most insurers have an 0800 helpline for free advice – call them just in case.

o   Remember – some alterations will require permission from the local authority.

Whether you need local authority permission, and what kind of permission you need, depends on the kinds of changes you plan to make, and to some extent on where you live (is it in a conservation area or an Area of Outstanding Natural Beauty?) and whether or not your home is a listed building. Remember that even if you do not need planning permission for your project, you could still require building regulation approval. The next step, therefore, is to tell your local authority what alterations you have in mind.

It is easy to think of planning officers as a bunch of killjoys, but the planning system is intended to protect the interests of the environment and the community as a whole. In my experience, local authorities would like to say yes to your application, unless your project is likely to harm the character and amenity of your neighbourhood. To avoid falling foul of your local planning officials, make friends with them at the beginning. Your local authority will certainly offer free leaflets on the subject, and many now have websites too.

For a general explanation of what does and does not require planning or building regulation permission, try the DIY Doctor website: www.diydoctor.org.uk (see 'Useful contacts', p 75). This website lists the kinds of project that would and would not need permission, and also explains *why* you need to get permission.

Council tax considerations

Always let your local authority know that you are going to take in a **lodger**. If you receive council tax benefit, you will need to tell them anyway. Let us assume, however, that you do not receive council tax benefit. If you live alone, or if everyone else in your household is:

o   under 18;

o   a student; or

o   severely mentally impaired,

you will be receiving a 25% discount on your council tax. Taking in a lodger could affect this discount; it depends whether your lodger would normally have to pay council tax. In general, taking in a student or a young person under 18 will not affect your discount, although in the case of a student they will probably need to show the local authority some proof of their status.

Other lodgers might well lose you your discount; but if your lodger pays council tax somewhere else (as might be the case with someone working away from home), you may be able to keep your discount. Always call the council tax department of your local authority for advice.

Private home or a house in multiple occupation (HMO)?

In general, few local housing authorities would take an interest in an ordinary house with one or two **lodgers** living *en famille*. In areas where there is a heavy demand for accommodation, such as in university towns, they do not want to rock the boat. In fact, a senior official (who asked not to be named) begged me not to advise my readers to ask the local authority to be involved just for one lodger, or even for two!

However, if you take in more than three lodgers, the local authority could take the view that you are running an **HMO** – a house in multiple occupation. A legalistic definition of an HMO, taken from the website of the Office of the Deputy Prime Minister, is 'a house which is occupied by persons who do not form a single household'. It then goes on to define 'house', 'occupied' and 'single household', and most people are likely to get lost along the way.

The Chartered Institute of Environmental Health is more helpful. Read their list below, and see whether what you are providing might constitute an HMO:

Category A: houses occupied as individual rooms, where there is some exclusive occupation (usually bedroom or living room) and some shared amenities (bathroom/ WC/kitchen). Each occupant lives independently of all others.

Category B: houses where the occupants 'share' the dwelling. Members of a defined social group, for example, students or a group of young single adults, would normally occupy these buildings. The occupiers each enjoy exclusive use of a bedroom but would share other facilities, including a communal living space.

Category C: houses with some degree of shared facilities, occupied by people whose occupation of the building is ancillary to their employment or education. The housing is made available through an employer or in connection with a recognised educational establishment. This would typically be student 'halls of residence', nurses' residences or soldiers' barracks.

Category D: houses referred to as hostels, guesthouses, bed and breakfast hotels or the like. These provide accommodation for people with no other permanent dwelling as distinct from hostels that provide accommodation for temporary visitors to an area.

Category E: premises requiring registration under the Registered Homes Act 1984. These provide board and personal care for persons in need by reason of old age, disability, past or present mental disorders or drug or alcohol dependence.

Category F: most houses or other buildings that by erection or conversion comprise dwellings that are self-contained, but the dwellings have access via a single 'front door' from a common area. Such dwellings would normally contain all the standard amenities, but not necessarily. Nevertheless, there is no sharing of amenities with the occupiers of neighbouring dwellings.

A typical HMO, therefore, might be a large house divided into bedsits or flats, each occupied by a different individual or family. The law has little to say about **resident landlord**s and their lodgers. HMOs, however, are subject to health and safety restrictions which do not apply to ordinary single-family homes.

HMOs are covered by the Housing (Management of Houses in Multiple Occupation) Regulations 1990 and also the Housing Act 1990. Local authorities have a **statutory** obligation to operate registration schemes for HMOs and to make sure that the law is obeyed.

The landlord or manager of an HMO is responsible for repairing, maintaining and cleaning the public areas of the property, organising refuse disposal and keeping the gas, electricity, drains and water supplies in good order. Safety measures – especially fire safety – are obligatory too.

Shared housing is obviously a greater fire risk than single-family housing – think of several separate kitchen stoves, apart from anything else – and the local authority will insist you install whatever fire precautions their inspector judges necessary. These will probably include smoke alarms, fire extinguishers, special door closures, fire escapes and other fire safety measures to protect the residents from risk of death or injury, and signs showing escape routes in case of fire must be on display.

There must also be a notice on display where all the residents can see it, showing the name, address and telephone number of the person managing the HMO.

Councils will also be concerned about possible overcrowding, and will set a limit on the number of people allowed to live in the property.

If you think any of this might conceivably apply to you, speak to your local housing department at the outset, rather than risk falling foul of them later. Local authorities are happy to advise **landlord**s free of charge, and they will know from the description you give whether or not you have strayed into HMO country.

Even if you are totally sure you are not about to run an **HMO**, you should still consider asking your local fire prevention officer (FPO), whose number will be in your local telephone directory, to check out your home for fire safety. This service, which is available to all householders, whether owner-occupiers or tenants, will normally be free of charge. The FPO will probably let you have a written report. Read it carefully and act on it. A fire blanket by the kitchen stove and a smoke alarm on the landing cost very little – some local fire departments even provide them either free of charge or at reduced prices – and could save lives.

Are you insured?

Your insurers – of both buildings and contents – will want to know what you are up to. Tell them in writing that you are planning to take in a **lodger**, and keep a copy (you will find a sample letter in 'Notices and letters' (p 67) and on the companion website).

Do not take in a lodger until you have your insurers' go-ahead. If you do not tell your insurance company, they may refuse to pay out on a claim, such as for a fire caused by your lodger's negligence. Your lodger's **deposit** will not go far if they burn your house down!

Your lodger may want to take out insurance for their own possessions, especially valuable items such as computers, hi-fi equipment, etc. You may be able to combine this with your own home contents insurance policy; ask your insurers what deals are available.

1. The good news: some insurers will give you a discount on your premiums if you ask the crime prevention officer (CPO) from your local police to advise on security in your home, and then put in place the measures he advises. These might include deadlocks on doors, a security light over the front door, and window locks (which are cheap to buy and extremely simple to install). The advice is free, and you sometimes get a special deal on the equipment too. This advice, of course, applies whether you take in a lodger or not.

2. More good news: some insurers will give you a small discount on your buildings and contents premiums if you install basic fire safety precautions. Smoke alarms cost just a few pounds each and they are very easy to install. This, too, applies whether you take in a **lodger** or not.

The bad news: some contents insurance policies have in their small print a fiendishly cunning get-out clause which means you will not be compensated for theft from your property unless entry has been forced. The insurance company may therefore avoid paying out in the event of theft by your **lodger** (who, of course, has a key!). The moral is, therefore, to choose your lodger with care, but the risk is still there.

As well as protection against any damage your **lodgers** may do, make sure you have insurance against claims by lodgers which may arise if they are injured as a result of defects in your property or contents. A loose piece of stair carpet could cost you dearly. Check your insurance policy carefully – most ordinary household policies will cover this situation. The buzzword is 'Third Party Liability'. If in doubt, call your insurers' free helpline.

Practical points

Apart from being 'habitable' in the legal sense, the accommodation you give your **lodger** needs to combine attractiveness with durability – is it fair to offer anyone accommodation you yourself would not like to live in? Besides, who would want to pay good money to live there?

o   Consider ease of maintenance; and

o   look to the long term.

There may be second-hand bargains to be had in salerooms or through the small ads of your local newspaper. Check out the notice boards in supermarkets and the postcards in shop windows. Why buy a new chest of drawers, for example, if you can get a second-hand one in good condition for £20? I once bought a superb bookshelf for £15 from a lady who was doing up her house and had more money than sense.

Here are my top tips. If you know all about them already, please feel free to move on to the next section.

Floor covering

o   Choose floor covering which will wear well and keep its good looks for a long time. Very cheap floor coverings are a false economy because they will soon get shabby.

o   When calculating the cost of fitted carpets, remember to include the price of the underlay, grippers and the fitter's time. Do not try to fit floor coverings yourself unless you *really* know what you're doing.

o   If money is short, you may be better off buying good quality carpet or vinyl second-hand (it's amazing how many people dispose of nearly-new items for almost nothing) and paying a professional to fit it.

o   If the floorboards are in reasonable condition, consider sanding and polishing them and spending the money you have saved on a couple of attractive rugs (again second-hand if you can find them).

Décor

o   Keep the décor simple, inexpensive and neutral. You and your lodger may not share the same tastes!

o   Emulsion paint (look for a finish which shrugs off fingermarks and scuffs) is cheaper than wallpaper for walls, and far easier to apply and renew.

o   Always keep left-over paint (clingfilm under the lid stops it from drying up) for future retouching.

Pictures

Either:

o   have an agreement with your lodger ('You may put up pictures and posters provided you make good before you leave'); or

o   put up some old-fashioned picture rail (available by the metre from a DIY shop) to enable your lodger to put up pictures without damaging your walls.

Beds, bedding and soft furnishings

Provide the best bed you can afford. You may never have slept in your spare bed, and your visitors may have been too polite to tell you how uncomfortable it is. The small ads are a good source of nearly-new beds as well as other furniture. More points:

o   Always fit a waterproof mattress cover. We aren't necessarily talking incontinence here; coffee or Ovaltine is just as harmful to mattresses!

o   A bed with drawers underneath is useful if you are short of space.

o   Thoroughly launder duvets and pillows, or even better, buy new ones.

o   Avoid feather fillings; many people are allergic to them.

o   Charity shops are a good source of nearly-new bed linen and curtains. Choose neutral, inoffensive designs and steer clear of anything that needs a lot of ironing.

Furniture and equipment

Keep it simple; keep it unisex! Some useful points:

o   A desk or computer workstation is a must, together with a suitable chair. Once again, check out the small ads.

o   Provide plenty of space for books.

o   Provide plenty of storage space for clothes, etc.

o   Always buy small electrical items such as kettles, toasters, bedside lamps, etc, new to avoid potential accidents – and keep the instructions and proofs of purchase in a safe place.

o   Good lighting is important, especially if your lodger spends a lot of time at a desk.

I know **landlords** who make a point of spending 24 hours in their letting accommodation to make sure that nothing is missing (desk or table for writing? Bookshelf? Bedside lamp?) and that everything works. It saves time and trouble in the long run.

3

Finding a lodger

Before you start looking for a likely **lodger**, here is a word of warning. Forget the clichés – there are exceptions to every rule except one: *never take in friends and relations!* You, of course, will know the individuals better than I do, but ask yourself:

o   Can I put the transaction on a business-like footing and keep it that way?

o   Can I be as firm with them as with a stranger, such as in insisting on regular rent payments and observance of house rules?

o   Can I be sure of getting rid of them when the time comes?

Unless the answer to all three questions is a resounding *yes*, find a good excuse for turning them down without hurting their feelings.

Setting a fair rent

If you know someone who takes in **lodgers**, you may already be familiar with the going rate in your neighbourhood. If your own network of friends fails to come up with any answers, however, do some research. Check out other people's advertisements in your local newspaper and on notice boards.

Even better, you can approach the people who can send you potential lodgers (see 'Promising sources of likely lodgers', p 22). They match lodgers to **landlords** on a daily basis and they can tell you what the going rate is for the kind of accommodation you are offering. So when you make friends with a student housing officer, personnel officer or whatever, find out what rent you should be charging. Say exactly what you are offering and ask them what their clients would expect to pay. Then set your rent accordingly.

Likely lodgers

Why, given that **lodgers** have less legal protection than a tenant would have, does anyone choose to become a lodger? For many people, the obvious attraction is the absence of a minimum stay. An assured shorthold tenancy, which is the agreement under which most houses and flats are let, specifies a minimum period of at least six months. During that period, the tenant is obliged to pay the rent even if they do not occupy the premises. There are many people who do not know where they will be or what they will be doing in six months' time and therefore cannot realistically take on such a commitment, so they go into digs for as long as they need to.

Here are just a few examples of people who become lodgers by choice or through force of circumstances. You can probably think of several more for yourself:

o   people working away from home;

o   students and trainees;

o   people separated from their partners and having some time out while deciding what to do next;

o   people house hunting or saving up to buy their own homes;

o   people receiving state benefits, whose entitlement will not stretch to a place of their own;

o   people who have extra support needs which make it more difficult for them to cope living entirely on their own.

Promising sources of likely lodgers

Three organisations that are likely to be looking for lodgings are:

o   **University/college accommodation offices**

They may well be looking for accommodation for staff and researchers as well as students – ask. In any case, they are likely to keep a central register of property. Adding your name to their database is usually free – though do check this before you go ahead. The student accommodation office may have a notice board where you can pin a postcard and the accommodation officers may be willing to pass on a handout of your details (but take care how much information you give out – see below). Some universities or colleges inspect prospective lodgings before they put you on their list, while others are simply glad of another address to hand out to clients.

○ **Hospitals**

There never seems to be enough accommodation for nurses and doctors and, as with universities and colleges, there will probably be an official who will be glad to add you to their database. See above.

○ **Personnel departments of big employers in your area**

They will usually be delighted to put you on their database or display a card on their notice board. Many will want short term accommodation for employees who are new to the area. Industries with highly mobile workforces are a prime target.

It is sometimes possible to have an arrangement with one of these organisations, rather than with an individual **lodger**. In this case, the accommodation office would be responsible for the rent and you would liaise with them, not with your lodger, over any points that arose. It isn't possible to generalise; you will need to call the organisation concerned and ask whether they offer such arrangements.

Other ways of finding a lodger include:

○ word of mouth (but avoid close friends and relations – see the warning above);

○ the local housing authority;

○ an advertisement in a newspaper or magazine read by the kind of person you hope to attract;

○ the 'Accommodation Wanted' section of the local newspapers and free sheets;

○ cards in shop windows or on supermarket notice boards.

Planning your advertising

Advertisements in a local newspaper or magazine (national ones would cast your net too wide) can be expensive, but you do reach a larger readership. Start by looking at other people's ads in the property section of your local newspaper and noting the accepted abbreviations that will save you money.

You should give all or most of the following information:

o approximate location;

o any obvious selling points such as 'quiet', 'own shower', 'private parking' (usually abbreviated to 'pte pkg'), 'use of gdn' or 'nr shops';

o rent expected, adding 'exc' if your **lodger** will be responsible for utility bills and 'inc' if they will not;

o any special points, such as 'Refs reqd' (references required), or 'Quiet N/S prof' (quiet, non-smoking professional person);

o contact telephone number, box number or possibly e-mail address.

Draft an advertisement that seems OK to you – remember that this is your first contact with your potential lodger, so it might pay you to spend money on a word or two saying how attractive your proposed accommodation is. Then call the advertising department of your chosen publication and find out:

o the deadline – if the property section of your local newspaper comes out on a Friday, you may need to submit your ad by Wednesday noon. Don't miss the boat; and

o the cost – some telesales people are on commission and will try to sell you an elaborate package you don't need, such as a free insertion if you pay for three. One insertion in the right place at the right time will usually be enough.

You may be able to dictate the advertisement over the telephone, paying by credit card. If so:

o always ask them to send a copy of the invoice for your file;

○ make sure you spell out anything potentially confusing, and have the telesales person repeat the entire ad to you, especially the contact details.

You can usually get a free insertion in the next issue if they make a big mistake, such as getting your telephone number wrong, but their carelessness could lose you a week's rent. You are unlikely to be able to claim any lost rent from them; their terms and conditions will almost certainly exclude this, though it is always worth checking!

---

1   When advertising in a newspaper or magazine, it is a good idea to ask for a box number if you are not in a tearing hurry. A box number costs a little extra, but it avoids nuisance telephone calls because candidates have to write to the box number and the newspaper then passes the letters to you. Your telesales person will tell you how to do this.

2   If you have e-mail – and if you expect your potential **lodgers** to have e-mail too – add your e-mail address. Like a box number, it avoids nuisance telephone calls.

3   If you have access to a fax line, quote the fax number in your advertisement. That way you get a written communication from your potential lodger.

4   A handout or a card for a notice board will need to be both legible and presentable. Typing or printing is better than a handwritten notice unless your writing is totally legible.

First contact

This is a wicked old world. Looking on the black side, we have all heard of criminals answering accommodation advertisements as part of their preparations for future burglaries. There are also some sad, unstable people who call the numbers in the small ads and then say obscene or threatening things over the telephone. There have also been cases of **lodgers** committing criminal offences against the persons and property of their **landlords** (in May 2001, a lodger received a life sentence for murdering his landlady!).

Anyone who takes in a lodger is accepting a certain amount of risk; risk that begins even before your lodger crosses the threshold. You can at least minimise the risk by being sparing with the information you give out in any advertisements (see above) and by finding out what you can about your prospective lodger's personal history and background before you meet them face to face.

To protect yourself, consider some or all of the following:

o   Be aware that not all callers may be looking for lodgings, and that some villains can be very plausible.

o   Never give your full address in any advertisement – a contact number or e-mail address is enough.

o   When someone rings to enquire about your accommodation, write down whatever telephone number they give you, then ring 1471 afterwards to check that the two numbers are the same. If they aren't, there may be a harmless explanation but, on the other hand, there may not.

o   Avoid giving any personal information – such as the fact that you live alone – in your advertisement or on the telephone.

o   Don't answer late night telephone calls. People can call again at a reasonable hour or forget the whole thing.

o   If the call turns obscene or malicious, resist the temptation to burst into tears (they'll love it) or make wisecracks (they'll call you again to see if you can keep it up). Just put down the receiver, do a swift 1471 in case they've been careless, and in any case tell both your telephone company and the police.

o   Don't give a candidate your address until you are sure you want to meet them.

o   Before meeting a candidate always call them at home or at work to make sure they are still intending to turn up – 'no shows' are a waste of time.

o   Listen to your inner voice. If you don't like the sound of them, don't meet them face to face.

o   Try to arrange for a friend or, if you have one, your dog, to be with you when you do meet candidates. Your friend can check them out as well, and if your normally benign hound growls and goes all stiff-legged, ask yourself why.

Checking out your lodger

Inviting someone to live with you in your own home is a very personal matter. Taking in a **lodger** on the spur of the moment is like marrying in haste – you may find yourself repenting at leisure. Once a candidate gets past first base (see above), take time to interview them carefully.

Your ideal lodger?

You are looking for someone who will:

o   pay the rent;

o   be considerate in using any shared parts of your home;

o   get along with you, your family and possibly your pets.

Horror stories apart, you need to be clear in your own mind about the house rules you will set – and enforce. For example:

o   Would you reject a smoker out of hand?

o   What about music in the evenings?

o   How do you feel about visitors?

This person is going to live under your roof and you have every right to turn down anyone you find uncongenial or who you think might cause annoyance to you or your neighbours (though see 'No discrimination!', p 31). It is sensible to write down a list of all the possible areas of disagreement; you are the person best placed to do this.

Your checklist

I tend to sift candidates as we talk on the telephone, making notes on a checklist that I keep in my file. You will probably find it helpful to do the same and I have provided a sample checklist below.

Always use a fresh sheet of paper for each caller. It is surprisingly easy to mislay people's details unless you are organised. You may find yourself rejecting several hopefuls before you actually make an appointment to show anyone around. This is to be expected. You may also find that an apparently perfect candidate turns into a pumpkin; if you keep good records you will be able to contact the other people on your file.

First telephone contact with prospective lodger (example)

Candidate's name ....

Home address ....

Contact details:

Home ....

Work ....

E-mail ....

Working? [   ]   Student? [   ]   On benefits? [   ]

Can they give references? [   ]

Deposit available? [   ]

Where were they living before? ....

Any other information they volunteer about themselves

....

Arrange to show around? [   ]

Put on backup list? [   ]

Not suitable? [   ]

The interview

If you have not done much interviewing before, consider having a dry run with a friend playing the part of a prospective **lodger**.

- Consider asking for identification (driver's licence? Passport?) at the start.
- Never try to interview in a hurry.
- Put your telephone on answerphone mode and give each candidate your full attention.
- Allow plenty of time for each prospective lodger.
- Allow a pause between candidates to enable you to make notes while everything is fresh in your mind.

Have each candidate's first contact details in front of you (see above). You might even consider producing a formal Lodger Application Form for candidates to fill in. I haven't gone quite so far, but you can find one on the *Landlordzone* website (see 'Useful contacts', p 75).

Prepare a list of points to mention. You may like to start with the checklist below and add any special points of your own.

Try also to envisage the kinds of questions you are likely to be asked and have your answers ready.

Here is a checklist of points to consider:

- Are you prepared to accept a lodger receiving state benefits? [ ]

  (See Chapter 4 before saying no.)

- Are you satisfied that your prospective lodger will be able to pay the rent? [ ]

  We're not talking about demanding a complete statement of means here, just some indication that there is enough money coming in from a reliable source. An employer's reference should help here.

- Has your prospective lodger got either the **deposit** or the means to obtain it? [ ]

  Remember, there are **deposit guarantee schemes** to help **housing benefit** clients with deposits (see p 44 for details).

- Is your prospective lodger likely to be clean, tidy and punctual? [ ]

  This is just a personal view, but I would think carefully before accepting anyone who turned up late for their interview without a good reason, wearing anything other than clean clothes and 'shining morning face'. The unpunctual, scruffy ones may be warm, wonderful people but I don't want to share my house with them. You are, of course, welcome to disagree.

o   Is your prospective lodger being frank and forthcoming with you? [   ]

Beware of anyone who seems unwilling to talk about their employer, their previous **landlord**, etc. You will, of course, in any case ask for references – *and follow them up without fail* (see 'References', p 32).

o   Remember that the rent, which you have set after carefully researching the going rates for your area (see p 21), is not negotiable. If a prospective lodger wants to haggle, turn them down flat.

o   Make clear your views on matters such as:

   –   smoking;

   –   pets;

   –   visitors;

   –   use of washing machine;

   –   kitchen rights;

   –   access to your telephone;

   –   the lodger's own electrical equipment (you could insist on an electrical safety check before letting it into your home), etc,

and stick to your guns. This is your home and you call the shots.

o   Is there anything about the prospective lodger that might annoy you or your neighbours? Do not, for example, accept a lodger who is learning the saxophone unless you either live in a detached house or are sure everyone in the street will appreciate the music.

o   Be businesslike, but listen to your own gut reactions too. If there seems something faintly dodgy about a prospective lodger, something you can't quite put your finger on, there is probably a good reason. Trust your intuition. You will not often be wrong.

Remember, they'll be checking *you* out too!

Do remember that your potential lodgers, while you are assessing them, will be checking you out too. Several websites (notably universities and colleges) advise potential lodgers on finding the perfect **landlord** and give lists of leading questions to ask ('Does the loo flush properly? When was the wiring last checked? Who are the neighbours and are they noisy?'). It is worth accessing one of these websites.

Be ready when the doorbell rings and make sure your home – and especially the accommodation the lodger will occupy – looks as attractive and as welcoming as possible.

Some candidates may have several places to view. You may like to give each one a small typed or printed handout to remind them what you are offering. Include:

o   address;
o   rent;
o   **deposit**; and
o   your contact telephone number and/or e-mail address.

Accepting and rejecting

Never decide on the spot, however strong your gut feeling about someone is. Say 'I'll let you know', name a day or time to call them, and *keep your promise.*

No discrimination!

Never turn away a prospective **lodger** *solely* on grounds of:

o   race;
o   nationality;
o   colour; or
o   religion.

Racial discrimination, in particular, is against the law. Even if you draft a racially discriminatory advertisement, no responsible newspaper will publish it.

Although the Discrimination Act 1995 does not apply to **resident landlords** letting accommodation in their own home, you should still not turn away a prospective lodger on grounds of race. Apart from the fact that you might be turning down the perfect lodger, you would be encouraging racism. Of course, there are many perfectly acceptable reasons for turning someone down – bad references, for example.

Be nice

In turning people down, be kind and tactful. Nobody likes to feel rejected. Emphasise how difficult it was to make your choice. The unsuccessful candidates will inevitably talk to their friends and colleagues and you would prefer them to speak well of you!

When you call your chosen **lodger** to inform them of their good fortune, you must tell them that the deal is subject to satisfactory references (see below).

Never worry about possible loss of income if it takes you a while to find your perfect **lodger**. It is better to have a lean couple of weeks while you seek out the perfect lodger than to install one in a hurry and regret it later.

References

Once you have made your choice, it is time to do some serious checking. However charming your prospective lodger seems, the two key questions are always:

o   Can your lodger pay the rent?

o   Will your lodger look after your property?

Nothing can guarantee a 'yes' to either of these questions, but you can reduce the risks by:

o   asking for references;

o   following them up;

o   taking a **deposit** (see below).

Do not rely on references that the lodger hands you without checking them thoroughly.

As an example of what can happen, a colleague of mine once interviewed a prospective lodger whose glowing testimonial, supposedly from the director of the haulage firm for whom the lodger was a transport manager, turned out to be bogus. To be precise, the headed paper was genuine, the lodger was who he said he was, but when my colleague telephoned the director he had never given such a reference. The prospective lodger had typed and signed the document himself. If my colleague had been lax about checking him out, she could have let a liar and a cheat into her home.

I suggest asking for:

○ a financial reference, such as from an employer (is your lodger's job secure?) or a bank;

○ a reference from a previous **landlord** (why did they leave?);

○ a personal reference from a responsible person who has known your prospective lodger for at least three years.

Always, always, always take up the references.

There is a sample reference request in 'Notices and letters' (p 69) and on the companion website. Always enclose a stamped, addressed envelope if you are expecting a reply by post.

Some referees will be more forthcoming over the telephone than in a letter. Listen carefully and note any hesitation or too-careful choice of words. Nobody likes to speak ill of anyone, but there are ways of leaving things unsaid. For example, 'Henry was – er – very gregarious' could mean that Henry held wild parties at unsociable hours.

4

Lodgers receiving state benefits

Be open-minded

If you have set your heart on a **lodger** with the right connections and a well paid job, you can skip this section. Do, however, try to avoid stereotyping people. Most people receiving state benefits would much rather be paying their own way, and if you have ever been in difficulties yourself you may wish to help someone else who has fallen on hard times.

There is a particular demand for lodgings for people receiving benefits who:

o   are aged between 16 and 25, whose entitlement will not cover the rent of a place of their own;

o   are divorced or separated;

o   have extra support needs of some kind which make it hard for them to cope with living entirely on their own.

There are three likely sources of such potential lodgers:

o   an advertisement in your local newspaper, especially if you add 'DSS OK';

o   your local authority housing department;

o   local homelessness charities and similar organisations.

By going through housing organisations you may find the people in most urgent need. Not all areas are equally well served in this respect. In my experience, the national homelessness organisations such as Shelter tend to be geared more to giving general advice than to actually finding accommodation for individuals. There are, however, some wonderful local initiatives, often operating on a shoestring. There may be one near you.

In my own area, the Coastal Housing Action Group (CHAG) works hand-in-hand with the local authority and benefits agencies to match **landlords** with prospective lodgers and tenants.

CHAG's relationship with landlords is exemplary.

ɔ   They will take careful note of the landlord's requirements and can often arrange for you to meet a selection of prospective lodgers.

ɔ   They will lend a hand with form-filling for candidates in receipt of benefits.

ɔ   They may be able to provide **deposits** from their own funds or from related charities. This is a thing no local authority, however helpful otherwise, is likely to do (though see the **deposit guarantee scheme**, p 44).

ɔ   They are often able to advance the first month's rent while the lodger's **housing benefit** is churning through the system. I have not yet found a local authority that will pay rent up front, and some take a long time to process your lodger's claim.

Potential lodgers don't need to be claiming benefits to consult organisations like CHAG; many people in good jobs who are new to the area consult CHAG or its equivalent rather than an agent who may charge them extortionate fees for poor service.

To see what your local CHAG equivalent is, approach your local Citizens Advice Bureau (CAB) for details of organisations operating in you area.

Under-18s and adults with learning difficulties

Many social services departments are desperate to find what are often called 'supported lodgings' for 16–18 year olds and other people who are in the care system. Legally, young people under 18 (and also people with learning difficulties) need special handling because they cannot make legally binding agreements. The buzzword here is 'guarantor' – an adult to guarantee that you will get paid.

In practice, with supported lodgings the contract is with the local authority, not the young person, so you are sure of your rent. Also, if you provide some support as well as accommodation, the rent you receive is higher than it might otherwise be. Ask your local social services department or charity what schemes they operate.

How much rent will you get?

By now you may be eager to take in a **lodger** receiving benefits. Well, there is a down side too. A local authority may not pay as much rent as a private lodger would (but see supported lodgings, above). The buzzword here is **'housing benefit'**. You can find out more about housing benefit on the Department for Work and Pensions website (www.dwp.gov.uk) but, broadly speaking, housing benefit is money paid to people on a low income (or no income at all) to help with payment of rent, and it is administered by the local authority. Housing benefit is strictly means tested, which means that a prospective lodger may not qualify for the full amount, not because the rent you are charging is excessive but because the lodger's income is too high.

Your prospective lodger has to claim housing benefit from the local authority. This involves filling in a detailed form and providing a copy of their Lodger Agreement.

How much housing benefit the local authority will pay for your lodger is based on two things:

o the lodger's age and entitlement (in assessing which their income and savings will be taken into account);

o what the local rent officer regards as the going rate for the accommodation you are offering.

You will already have set what you think is a fair rent (see 'Setting a fair rent', p 21) but the amount of housing benefit your lodger is offered may not be the same as the rent the private market will bear.

The local authority is likely to ask a rent officer to look at the rent you are charging in relation to what is called the 'local reference rent', which in the case of lodgings is the maximum amount the council will pay for a single room in a house. In theory, you can expect an official with a clipboard to knock on your door. In practice, the 'inspection' may simply be done in the office, based on a glance at the street map of your area and the rent officer's knowledge of the going rate for the kind of deal you are offering.

It is worth asking your local CAB what the local reference rent is for your locality: it might even (you never know your luck) be higher than the rent you were thinking of charging.

Once this assessment has been done, the local authority has calculated your **lodger's housing benefit** entitlement and your lodger has moved in, you may face a longish wait for your money. I know **landlords** who have been kept waiting for months while the paperwork moved through the system. This is where the 'rent in advance' scheme offered by organisations like CHAG (see above) could come into its own. Ask about this.

Eventually, you and your lodger will each receive a notice from the local authority saying how much housing benefit will be paid each week. If you have set a monthly rent this might seem confusing, but it's quite straightforward if you can do simple arithmetic (or, even better, operate a calculator). Let's suppose you have set a rent of £350 per calendar month. That of course works out at £4,200 per year or £80.76 per week. The formula is:

Rent £350 per month

Multiply by 12 to get annual rent: £4,200

Divide by 52 to get weekly rent: £80.76

If you are lucky, your lodger's housing benefit entitlement will be the same as your rent. If there is a shortfall it is your responsibility to claim it from your lodger.

The money, when it eventually comes through, is usually paid four-weekly in arrears.

1   It is easier if you set a weekly rent so that **housing benefit** payments relate directly to the rent.

2   If you do charge by the week you must issue a rent book (see p 61).

At the time of writing, the housing benefit system is under review. The government is piloting a new system called the 'standard local housing allowance' which, in theory at least, will do away with much of the bureaucracy of the current system.

The idea is to have a set amount of money available in each area for housing costs, according to the size of the family. So a single person would be entitled to X, a couple to Y, a couple with a child to Z, and so on. The claimant would then know in advance how much money they were entitled to, and could look for accommodation at or around that price. If they could find something for less money they would be allowed to keep the difference; if the accommodation was more expensive, they would have to make up the difference. The new system is being piloted in 10 different areas, due to start in October 2003 and continuing until April 2004. If all goes well, the government will bring in legislation to change the whole housing benefit system.

Direct payment of rent

If you do take a **lodger** who qualifies for **housing benefit**, you can (with the Lodger's Agreement – you will be given a special form for you both to sign) arrange for the rent to be paid directly to you. If a lodger receiving housing benefit gets behind with the rent, the housing authority can choose to pay you direct anyway, but as there usually was to be at least eight weeks' arrears, you may prefer to be paid direct from the beginning.

Direct payment of rent can be a splendid thing, but see 'Clawing back overpayments', p 40, before you sign up for it.

Coping with officialdom

This is not a book about local authorities, but it is worth mentioning that officials can and do lose documents and then deny ever having received them. This is usually due to the 'If I can't find it on the computer system it doesn't exist' phenomenon rather than to deliberate deceit.

I have said that many local authorities take a long time to come up with any money. This is because there is a lot of documentation involved. It can take many working days to transfer the information on a stack of **housing benefit** forms onto the local authority's computer system. Forms have been known to go missing before their details have been entered, and people can and do make typing errors in transferring your information to their database. Of course, the inconvenience for you is the same whatever the reason for the hiccup. In your dealings with officialdom it pays to make sure your record keeping is better than theirs! So:

- o keep a file labelled 'LODGER';
- o make a note of any reference number or code allocated to your case; write this on the file, and quote it in every communication – both by telephone and in writing – with the authority;
- o keep a copy of everything you send or hand in;
- o keep careful notes for your file of all telephone conversations, with dates and the name of the official you spoke to;

    (You think you will remember what was said: believe me, in a month's time you will have forgotten all about it!)
- o get a signed receipt for everything you hand in;
- o if it is practicable, make friends with an official connected with your case. I say 'if this is practicable': I live in a rural area and this advice works for me, but in urban areas with huge call centres you may never speak to the same person twice. If you do get someone's name and job title, write this on the front of the file and call them regularly to ask about progress.

Clawing back overpayments

Having your **lodger's housing benefit** paid straight to you can work very well. You can have the money paid by standing order straight into your bank account and you will usually be sent a written record of each payment, which helps you to keep good records.

But beware! Let us suppose that your lodger, for whatever reason, receives more housing benefit than they are entitled to. If the money has been paid to your lodger, the local authority will chase *them* for the overpayment, not you.

If housing benefit has been paid direct to you, however, the local authority – *even if you yourself are totally unaware of anything untoward* – will claw back the overpayment not from your lodger, but from *you*.

The local authority have the **statutory** power to recover this money from you and, because they are generously rewarded by central government for doing so, they will do their utmost to exercise that power!

They will do this either by demanding payment from you there and then, or by deducting the overpayment in instalments from the ongoing rent. If you don't pay, the local authority have the power to take you to court for the money, and recent case law indicates that they will win. A county court judgment against you would affect your future credit rating. It is, of course, grossly unfair to an innocent **landlord**, but that is what will happen.

You are then supposed to claim the money back from your lodger, but this is stressful at best and costly at worst. Suppose you get a county court judgment against your lodger: you may still never see your money. You can't get blood out of a stone! The judge will take the lodger's income into account and may order them to pay off their debt in such small instalments that you might as well have written off the money in the first place.

This is a worst-case scenario, and if you choose your lodger carefully it may never happen to you!

5

Deposits

It is important to ask your **lodger** for a **deposit** in addition to the first month's rent. This:

o is a useful test of a private lodger's financial soundness;

o reminds your lodger to behave; and

o gives you some protection if the lodger lets you down.

At the end of your lodger's stay, this sum can be used to:

o cover any unpaid rent;

o pay the cost of cleaning the property (unless, of course, cleaning is part of the deal); and

o make good any damage the lodger has done.

There is no upper or lower limit set by law, but one or two months' rent would be normal. The deposit (or what is left after any deductions you have to make for repairs, cleaning, etc) should be returned to the lodger at the end of their stay. Always give the lodger a receipt for their deposit. You will find a sample receipt in 'Notices and letters' (p 71) and on the companion website.

Keep it safe

Remember that a **deposit** is the **lodger's** money, not yours. You might have recourse to it in future, but for the moment you must not touch it. It is wise, therefore, to put your lodger's deposit in an account that is separate from your own finances. Who gets any interest on the money is a matter to be agreed between you and your lodger.

Ordinary high street banks pay a derisory rate of interest. Others offer a better deal, as you can see by checking out the 'Money' section in your newspaper.

For starters, Smile (www.smile.co.uk) is part of the Co-operative Bank and operates on the internet only, although you can pay money in at any post office and draw money out at any cashpoint. At the time of going to print, Smile was paying 3.75% gross on savings accounts. Intelligent Finance (www.if.com) is a telephone and internet banking service organised by the Halifax. At the time of going to print it offered 3.8% gross on savings accounts. A useful feature of Intelligent Finance is its scheme which enables you to keep money in several different 'pots' with names chosen by you. You might consider opening one of these with your lodger's first name and keeping the monthly statement in your file (see p 61 for advice on good record keeping).

I know a few **landlords**, myself included, who pick accounts that pay a good rate of interest and then pass on to their departing lodgers the interest their deposits have earned, but this is, of course, optional. I do find, however, that it encourages lodgers to behave!

Deposits for lodgers receiving state benefits

You may think that **deposits** would be out of the question for **lodgers** receiving benefits (see above) but you would be wrong.

As I said, many local authorities run a **deposit guarantee scheme** for lodgers and tenants claiming benefits. Typically, the local authority gives the **landlord** a guarantee or bond (not actual money – see below) to cover a maximum of one month's rent. The bond is handed to the landlord instead of a cash deposit. In return for this, the lodger pays a small sum – typically £5 or £10 – to the local authority and promises:

o   to pay the rent promptly;

o   not to cause any damage;

o   to pay the council for any damage that is caused.

If there is any damage at the end of the lodger's stay, the local authority – not the lodger – pays the landlord. The local authority then tries to recover the cost from the lodger and meanwhile you will have had your money.

Additionally, some housing charities can arrange deposits either from their own funds or from other charities (see the description of the Coastal Housing Action Group, p 36). Your local Citizens Advice Bureau will have lists of charities operating in your area.

Ex-services charities such as Forces Help can sometimes provide deposits for old comrades who have fallen on hard times. They may treat the deposit as a gift to the individual, not a loan, which means that if you have to use the deposit the charity will not ask you for their money back.

6

Your Lodger Agreement

Agreeing the terms

First of all, you and your prospective **lodger** need to agree everything on this checklist:

o the amount of rent;

o whether this will be paid weekly or monthly;

o how it will be paid, such as in cash or by cheque or standing order;

o the amount of **deposit**;

o whether your lodger will be responsible for any utilities (see 'A note on utilities', p 48);

o whether your lodger will use your telephone and, if so, how they will pay for their calls (in an ideal world your lodger will have their own mobile phone);

o the notice period – how much warning you will give the lodger if you want them to leave, and vice versa;

o what your lodger proposes to do about insuring their own possessions (you might be able to combine this with your own household policy (see p 15 for more information));

o the contents of the accommodation, and their condition (use an **inventory** that the lodger checks and signs (see the sample inventory in 'Notices and letters', p 55));

o what services, if any, you will provide (for example, cleaning, cooking, bed linen).

You will want to incorporate all the information above in your final agreement.

A note on utilities

You don't want all your rent gobbled up by enormous electricity and gas bills. Some people feel the cold more than others. You might be lucky enough to find a **lodger** reared in the 'Don't put a heater on, put a sweater on' school, but don't count on it!

Here are three options:

o   Consider making your lodger's rent exclusive of electricity and/or gas. When the next bill arrives, show it to your lodger together with an old bill for the same quarter, point out the difference and ask politely for a contribution.

o   Have an electricity or gas meter installed in your lodger's accommodation. Your own supplier will be able to do this. Modern meters take pre-payment cards, available at most post offices. They are, however, an expensive way of buying power and require a certain amount of forethought – what if the lights go out when the post office is closed?

o   Include lighting and heating in the rent, making sure you do not sell yourself short. In that case, consider agreeing a 'winter supplement' to cover extra heating costs.

Note that the Lodger Agreement (p 50) and on the companion website contains an optional clause to provide for your lodger to pay for separately metered services. If this does not apply to you, you will, of course, delete that clause.

The Lodger Agreement

You will see that the Agreement itself is quite a short document but it comes with a long list of 'standard provisions'.

The Lodger Agreement is specific – it is unique to you (whom we describe as the **Landlord** throughout) and your **lodger**. The standard provisions are, as the name implies, more general and because of that, there may be things in them that do not apply to your case. The standard provisions are important, however, because they set out the rules that you and your lodger are agreeing to abide by. It is important to read the standard provisions yourself, and to take time to talk them through with your lodger, before you both sign the Agreement.

Completing the paperwork

o Adjust the Lodger Agreement (p 50) to meet your needs, as above, and print out two copies.

o Adjust the **inventory** (p 55) to cover the accommodation and equipment you are providing and print out two copies.

o Fill in the Lodger Agreement in duplicate (one copy for you and one for the lodger), using the sample as a guide. Do everything except sign it.

Arrange a meeting with the lodger before they move in, and at the meeting:

o go through the Lodger Agreement and sign and date both copies;

o get the lodger to sign and date both copies (if you are to have more than one lodger, get everyone over 18 to sign);

o give the lodger one copy and keep the other;

o go through the inventory together and get the lodger to sign both copies (one for each of you);

o give the lodger their copy of your gas safety certificate (if any);

o collect the **deposit** (if any) and give a receipt;

o collect the first instalment of rent and give a receipt;

o hand over a key.

Lodger Agreement

Date:

The Landlord: *[your name and full address here]*

The Lodger: *[your **lodger's** name here]*

The Accommodation: *[describe the accommodation of which the lodger will have sole use]*

The Contents: as set out in the attached inventory *[and don't forget to attach one]*

The Shared Rooms: *[here you list shared accommodation, for example, kitchen, bathroom, utility room, etc; thoroughfares like hallways and staircases do not count as 'rooms']*

The Rent: £ *[insert amount here]*

Payable weekly/monthly in advance on the [ ] day of the week/month *[delete whichever does not apply]*.

Deposit: £ *[insert amount here]* to be paid on the signing of this Agreement with the Landlord.

Notice period: one week/one month/three months *[delete whichever does not apply]*.

A   The Landlord gives the Lodger the personal right to live in the Accommodation and to use the Shared Rooms with the Landlord/the Landlord's family *[delete whichever does not apply]*.

B The Lodger agrees to observe and perform the obligations set out in the Standard Provisions enclosed with this Agreement.

C This Agreement can be ended at any time:

  C1 by the Landlord giving the Lodger notice to quit the Accommodation at the end of the notice period;

  C2 by the Lodger giving the Landlord notice of his/her intention to vacate the Accommodation at the end of the notice period.

D The Landlord agrees to provide the following services: *[here you set out what you are prepared to offer, such as breakfast, cleaning, laundry, etc]*

E The Landlord's address for service of notices (including notices of proceedings) is the address given for the Landlord at the start of this Agreement.

Signed by the Landlord ....

Signed by the Lodger ....

Lodger Agreement: Standard Provisions

[The provisions contain a certain amount of 'law-speak'. I have added my own notes in italics at the end of each clause. It is sensible to take time to talk your lodger through the Agreement, referring to the notes and making sure everything is clear.]

1 Any restriction on the Lodger includes an obligation not to permit or allow an infringement by anyone visiting the Lodger.

 [The Agreement applies to anyone visiting the lodger as well as to the lodger him/herself.]

2 Words in the masculine are deemed to include the feminine and vice versa. The singular includes the plural and vice versa.

 [This avoids using 'he/she/they', 'him/her/them', etc. I wish I could do the same! I have tended to use

'they/them/their' in lieu of 'he/she, him/her and his/her'. If this irritates you, I apologise.]

3   If there is more than one Lodger, all their obligations can be enforced against all the Lodgers jointly and against each one individually.

[If, for instance, there are rent arrears and you have a single Agreement with a pair of lodgers, neither can avoid liability by claiming to have paid their share of the rent.]

4   The Landlord includes whoever for the time being owns the interest in the Property that gives a right to possession of it when the Lodger's right of occupation ends.

[This means that if you sell the house, or die, the new owner of the house steps into your shoes and the agreement remains in force (see 'FAQs', p xviii).]

5   The Lodger shall:

5.1   Pay the rent at the time and in the manner stated without any deduction.

[The lodger pays the amount set out in the Agreement, without deductions, at the time set out in the Agreement. If you want the rent to be paid by standing order, you can insist on this.]

5.2   Pay for telephone calls which the Lodger makes from the Landlord's Property.

[The lodger pays for their own phone calls if they use your telephone. Lodgers with mobile phones or private phones installed in their rooms are, of course, responsible for their own bills.]

5.3   Use the Accommodation for the Lodger to live in and no other purpose.

[This prevents the lodger using the property for business purposes. This is important because you will not qualify for the Rent-a-Room tax breaks (see p 62) otherwise.]

5.4   Keep the Accommodation clean and tidy.

5.5   Leave the Shared Rooms clean and tidy after use.

5.6   If supplies to the Accommodation are separately metered, arrange immediately with the relevant supply company for accounts for gas, electricity and telephone (if any) at the Accommodation to be addressed to the Lodger in his or her own name and pay all standing charges for these and all charges for gas and electricity supplied to the Accommodation and for telephone calls made from the Accommodation during the letting period.

[This clause may not apply to your case (see 'A note on utilities', p 48) and delete and re-number if necessary.]

5.7 Permit the Landlord to enter the Accommodation at any reasonable time.

[This is not intended as a snooper's charter, but allows you to get in for cleaning, repairs and, of course, in an emergency.]

6 The Lodger shall not:

6.1 Sell, hire out or remove the Contents.

[The lodger may not sell your sofa, donate your dresser or loan out your lawnmower.]

6.2 Deface or damage the Accommodation, any part of the Landlord's Property, or the Contents.

*[This stops the lodger putting up shelves, hammering picture hooks into the walls or scratching the table tops. Many **landlords** put up picture rails themselves and some agree to the use of sticky tape provided the lodger makes good afterwards (see p 18).]*

6.3 Play any live or electronic music, radio or TV or engage in any other noisy activity between such hours as the Landlord stipulates.

[This covers everything noisy that might annoy you or your neighbours: 11 pm to 8 am would be reasonable; this is something you must agree with your lodger.]

6.4 Keep anything dangerous or flammable at the Accommodation.

[No bombs, shotguns, chemistry sets, cans of petrol or portable Calor gas heaters.]

6.5 Keep animals in the Accommodation, except with the Landlord's prior written permission.

[You can treat each request on its merits.]

7 The Landlord holds the Deposit as security for compliance by the Lodger with his/her obligations, and the payment, holding and use of the Deposit

shall be without prejudice to any other right or remedy of the Landlord.

*[This allows you to hold the **deposit** and use it as you think proper (see Chapter 5).]*

7.1 If the Landlord shall need to have recourse to the Deposit whilst this Agreement continues, the Lodger shall immediately on demand pay the Landlord such amount as shall be required to restore the amount of the Deposit to the original sum.

[If you need to use part of the deposit, this clause enables you to make the lodger top it up again.]

7.2 The Deposit shall be repaid to the Lodger at the end of this Agreement less such part of it as the Landlord shall deem necessary to enable the Landlord to make good any breach of or non-compliance with the Lodger's obligations under this Agreement. If the Deposit shall be insufficient for this purpose the Lodger shall pay to the Landlord forthwith on demand such further sum as shall, in the opinion of the Landlord, be required.

[At the end of their stay the lodger gets the deposit back, less any amount that you have to spend to put right anything the lodger has done or failed to do. If the deposit is not enough to put things right, you can make the lodger pay the difference.]

8 If at any time any part of the rent is in arrears for 15 days (whether formally demanded or not) or any of the obligations on the Lodger's part are not observed and performed the Landlord may re-enter the Accommodation and this Agreement shall cease and determine.

[In this context 'determine' means 'terminate'. This is fairly draconian; you would, of course, try a gentle reminder first!]

Signed by the Landlord ....

Signed by the Lodger ....

The inventory

This sample **inventory** lists all the items in a spacious bed-sitting room with a kitchen area and its own shower room on the top floor of a large house.

It is an extremely comprehensive inventory. Do not be alarmed. Few **landlords** would equip their **lodger's** accommodation, especially the kitchen, so generously, but I have tried to think of everything you might consider supplying rather than miss anything out. You will wish to use my inventory as an *aide memoire* rather than as an instruction to go out and buy your lodger a pizza cutter! Delete anything you are not providing – and add anything extra to the list.

1   It is a good idea to specify the manufacturer of major items. I know a **landlord** whose **lodger** quietly swapped the microwave for an inferior model and took the expensive one away with her.

2   *Always* check electrical appliances before including them in the **inventory**. If it doesn't work reliably, you must repair or replace it. Always include instruction manuals in the inventory. If you have lost the instructions for something, it is worth contacting the manufacturer and asking for a fresh copy.

3   Remember to state the decorative condition of the accommodation and to add wording such as 'All items new or in very good condition unless otherwise stated'.

4   Your inventory should draw attention to any item that is shabby or damaged (the scorched carpet and discoloured Pyrex roasting dish, for example) so that nobody can blame the damage on your lodger.

Print out two copies, one for you and one for your lodger.

Sample inventory

All items new or in very good condition unless otherwise stated.

Kitchen area

Newly decorated
[Vinyl] flooring
[Strip] light fittings

[Slate grey] worktops

1 roller blind [or pair of curtains, or whatever]

1 [Zanussi] washer/dryer

Instructions for same

1 sink unit with [stainless steel] sink

1 [Phillips] [electric] cooker

Instructions for same

1 [Phillips] electric cooker hood

Instructions for same

1 [Whirlpool] fridge-freezer

Instructions for same

1 [Matsui] microwave cooker [with oven, grill and defrosting facilities]

Instructions for same

[　] wall cupboards

[　] low cupboards

[　] drawer units containing:

> [　] teaspoons
>
> [　] dessert spoons
>
> [　] dessert forks
>
> [　] table forks
>
> [　] large knives
>
> [　] small knives
>
> [　] serving spoons
>
> 1 apple corer
>
> 1 potato peeler
>
> 1 egg whisk,
>
> [　] wooden spoons
>
> [　] spatulas
>
> 1 pair of tongs,
>
> 1 potato masher
>
> 1 pizza cutter
>
> 1 pastry brush
>
> 1 pair of scissors
>
> 1 fish slice
>
> 1 bottle brush
>
> 1 strainer
>
> 1 grapefruit knife

            1 cook's knife,
            1 paring knife
            1 grater
            1 perforated spoon
            1 can opener
            1 corkscrew
1 [Morphy Richards] electric kettle
Instructions for same
1 saucepan rack with:
            1 milk pan
            1 large metal saucepan + lid
            1 glass large saucepan + lid
            1 glass small saucepan; no lid
            1 grill pan with holder
            1 non-stick frying pan
1 wall clock
1 vegetable rack
1 breakfast bar
[ ] stools
1 large waste bin
1 [Phillips] electric toaster
Instructions for same
1 [terracotta] coffee jar
1 set of [ ] [terracotta] storage jars
1 stand for kitchen roll
[ ] trays
1 mug tree with [ ] mugs
1 [white china] teapot
[ ] table mats
1 colander
1 plastic jug
1 coffee pot; [ ] filter cones; 1 packet of filter papers
[ ] plastic canister
1 [Pyrex] roasting dish [discoloured but sound]
[ ] tumblers
1 salt and pepper set
1 measuring jug

[ ] large dinner plates
[ ] small plates
[ ] bowls
1 washing up bowl
1 bucket
1 dustpan and brush
1 [Hoover upright] vacuum cleaner with tools
Instructions for same
1 packet spare vacuum cleaner bags
[ ] dusters
1 squeegee mop

Shower room

Newly decorated

[Vinyl] flooring

1 [pendant] light fitting with shade

1 roller blind

1 strip light over wash basin

1 shower cubicle containing [Texas] power shower

1 [chrome] shower caddy

1 [non-slip rubber] mat

1 [cotton] bathmat

1 wash basin

1 mirror

1 waste paper bin

1 shelf

1 linen bin

1 wall heater

1 soap dish

1 extractor fan

Bed-sitting room

Newly decorated
1 fitted carpet [slight scorch mark near window]

1 pendant light fitting with shade

1 [double] bed

1 [metal action] sofa bed

1 [pure wool] rug

[   ] scatter cushions

[   ] pairs of [glazed cotton] curtains [+ matching tie backs]

1 dining table

[   ] dining chairs [with glazed cotton seat cushions]

[   ] bookcases

1 desk

1 table lamp

1 typist's chair

1 coffee table

[   ] armchairs

1 [Phillips] TV and stand

Instructions for same

[   ] chests of drawers

1 waste paper bin

1 [electric storage] heater

Instructions for same

[   ] pictures

1 fitted wardrobe with shelves, containing:

    1 duvet

    [   ] pillows

    [   ] duvet covers

    [   ] bottom sheets

    [   ] pillowslips

    [   ] large towels

    [   ] small towels

We have thoroughly checked this inventory and agree that all is as set out above.

Signed by the Landlord   ....

Signed by the Lodger   ....

After the lodger moves in

Collecting the rent

You will have collected your first month's rent in advance. After that, a good **lodger** will pay the rent without being nagged. However, if you need to demand payment you MUST:

o   do so in writing; *and*

o   put your name and address on your demand,

otherwise it will not be valid (see the sample rent demand in 'Notices and letters' (p 72) and on the companion website).

Rent and record keeping

For **lodgers** who pay their rent *weekly* (or if your Lodger Agreement refers to a weekly amount), you are required by law to provide your lodger with a proper rent book. You can get this from any good stationers.

If yours is a *monthly* agreement, you are not required by law to provide a rent book. You will, of course, still have to keep good records of payments.

Here is a practical way of recording payments as well as other points that arise.

Buy a hardback notebook and enter inside the front cover the lodger's:

o   name;

- contact telephone no;
- date of arrival;
- amount of rent paid in advance;
- amount of **deposit** paid;
- date when rent is next due.

Then each time your lodger pays their rent, you enter on one side of the next double page spread the date and amount of rent paid, and sign it.

On the other side of the page you write about any points, major or minor, that have arisen during the month (for example, 'put up new curtains/replaced faulty toaster'), sign and date. Many **landlords** find this record very useful, especially for settling any disagreements.

Give your lodger a receipt for each month's rent (you will find a sample receipt in 'Notices and letters' (p 70) and on our website) and keep copies on file. Many landlords prefer to use a computer to generate the receipts and keep track of payments, but a receipt book with either carbon copies or stubs like a cheque book is just as good.

Beware of the **lodger** who offers to pay you in kind.

A spot of digging, dog-walking, baby-sitting or DIY is fine, provided the lodger is not breaking any rules by doing so. *There are strict rules about payments in cash or kind for lodgers receiving state benefits.* If in doubt, call your local benefits office (look in the telephone directory under 'Benefits') and ask about a hypothetical case.

A present from the taxman

Before 1995, you would have had to pay tax on any income you made from taking in a **lodger**. The good news, however, is that you may be in line for a present from the taxman!

It isn't often that the taxman gives anything away. However, the Inland Revenue's **Rent-a-Room scheme** was designed to increase the accommodation available for renting by encouraging people to rent out spare rooms in their homes.

Previously, potential **landlords** were nervous of doing this in case they were landed with a big tax bill. Under the Rent-a-Room scheme, they needn't worry unless they are grossing more than £4,250. Landlords do not need to be owner-occupiers to claim this allowance – council and housing association tenants are also eligible.

An Inland Revenue booklet, *Letting and Your Home* (IR87), is available explaining the scheme, but generally you should qualify for Rent-a-Room relief for a given tax year – that is, from 6 April of one year to 5 April the next – provided the accommodation you let during that tax year is:

o   furnished (the scheme does not apply to unfurnished accommodation);

o   for residential use (so renting out a room for someone to use as an office or workshop would not qualify for tax relief under the scheme);

o   in your only, or main, residence.

If you satisfy all these conditions, and if your *gross* rental income – that is, your income *before deducting your expenses* – from your lodger in any one tax year is not more than £4,250 (which comes to £354.16 per month or £81.73 per week), then that income is exempt from tax. If you and someone else – such as your partner – let the room jointly, you will each be entitled to half of the tax exemption – in other words, £2,125. If you have two lodgers, you will divide the allowance between them – £2,125 gross income per lodger.

There is a space to record Rent-a-Room income on your annual tax return. The taxman is not interested in the details. Unless your gross income from your lodger is more than £4,250 in the tax year concerned, all you need to do is tick the box and go on to the next section.

If your gross income from your lodger is more than £4,250, you can choose to pay tax *either*:

o   on your *net* profit (in other words, the *gross* rent less your expenses); *or*

o   on the part of the gross rent you receive which *exceeds* £4,250 (so if the gross rent was £5,000, you would be liable for tax on the extra £750 at whatever rate you would normally be liable for).

You do not, therefore, *have* to take part in the Rent-a-Room scheme if it is not to your advantage. Instead, you can ignore Rent-a-Room and simply declare all your income from your lodger and claim expenses and capital allowances against tax.

The free Inland Revenue leaflet (IR87), available from any tax office or on the Revenue's website (www.inlandrevenue.gov.uk), explains in detail how the scheme works and how to decide whether it is suitable for you.

8

Parting company

If you share essential accommodation with your **lodger**, there is no legal minimum notice period. Our sample Lodger Agreement (p 50, and on the companion website) gives you the option of one week, one month or three months.

Otherwise, the legal minimum is four weeks. In practice, you should give at least four weeks' notice to be both safe and friendly.

Most lodgers will leave when you ask them. If your lodger tries to dig their heels in, **serve** the Notice to Quit (see the sample in 'Notices and letters' (p 73) and on the companion website).

If the lodger refuses to budge at the end of the notice period, you have the right to evict them without taking them to court *if, but only if*:

o   *you share some essential accommodation* (such as kitchen, bathroom and/or lavatory – corridors and staircases don't count here) that is

o   in your *only or main* home

o   both *when your lodger moves in and at the time when you want them to go*.

Even so:

o   you *must* issue a proper Notice to Quit (see the sample in 'Notices and letters' (p 73));

o   you *must not* use or threaten physical violence.

Both unlawful eviction and harassment are criminal offences.

If you *do not* share 'essential accommodation' with your **lodger** and if they refuse to budge, you may not be able to evict them without a court order. This is not a DIY matter. Take professional advice.

If you move house

The bad news: if you move out of your home permanently (as opposed to going away for a few weeks on business or on holiday) and leave your **lodger** behind, you cease to be a **resident landlord** and your legal position changes drastically. You *must* therefore make sure that your lodger leaves when you do. If not, your lodger could become your tenant and gain **statutory** long term rights of residence.

The good news: the Lodger Agreement (see p 50) provides for whoever takes over from you to step into your shoes and become the **landlord**.

If for some reason you do want to leave your lodger behind when you move house (perhaps to look after the house/garden/pets while you work abroad), the answer is to grant them an assured shorthold tenancy (see *Letting Your Property* for details).

Student and holiday lettings

Students can be **lodgers** just like anybody else, but if, according to the criteria (see p 1) you are a non-**residential landlord**, you should read *Letting Your Property*.

Holiday lets are a different ball game altogether and are not covered in this book.

Notices and letters

Daffodil Cottage
Keswick
Cumbria

The Stardust Insurance Company
Stargazers Lane
London EC1

1 September 200[   ]

Dear Sirs

Policy No: WW/212/SGP/890/2

I have the above Property/the Contents of the above Property *[you will need to write separately to the insurers of both the buildings and the contents if there are two different insurance companies involved]* insured with you under the above policy.

I would like to inform you that I wish to take in a lodger. Will you please confirm that my Property/Contents insurance will continue in full force and effect during the letting, and that I will be fully insured in the event of:

damage to Property [Contents] by my lodger or my lodger's visitors;

theft of Contents by my lodger or my lodger's visitors;

injury or death of my lodger or damage to my lodger's belongings caused by defects in my Property [Contents].

I should also like your assurance that my existing third party cover will also extend to my lodger.

I would be grateful for your early reply and thank you in anticipation of your kind assistance.

Yours faithfully

William Wordsworth

Sample reference request

Daffodil Cottage
Keswick
Cumbria

to Mr PB Shelley
12 Skylark Rise
Crawley
Surrey

1 September 200[   ]

Dear Sir

I am considering taking in Mr Leigh Hunt as a lodger. Mr Hunt has given your name as a referee. I should be grateful if you would kindly tell me how long you have known him and in what capacity and let me have your views on his suitability as a lodger, including his ability to pay the rent and to keep my property in good order.

I thank you in anticipation of your assistance in this matter and attach a stamped, addressed envelope for your reply.

Yours faithfully

William Wordsworth

Sample receipt for rent

Date: 1 November 200[   ]

Landlord: John Keats

Property address: Endymion House
Nightingale Way
St Agnes
Cornwall

Lodger: Sam Coleridge

Amount: £350
Period: 1 November to 30 November 200[   ]

I acknowledge receipt of the amount above which is rent for the above period.

....
Landlord's signature

Sample receipt for deposit

Date: 1 November 200[   ]

Landlord: John Keats

Property address: Endymion House
                               Nightingale Way
                               St Agnes
                               Cornwall

Lodger: Sam Coleridge

Amount: £350

I acknowledge receipt of the amount above as deposit which I agree to hold on the terms of the Lodger Agreement between us of today's date.

....
Landlord's signature

Sample rent demand

Date: 1 November 200[   ]

Landlord: John Keats

Property address: Endymion House
                    Nightingale Way
                    St Agnes
                    Cornwall

Lodger: Sam Coleridge

Amount: £350
Period: 1 November to 30 November 200[   ]

Please make immediate payment of the amount stated above which is rent for the above period. Thank you.

....
Landlord's signature

....
date

Sample notice to quit

From: ....
[fill in your name and address here]
('The Landlord')

To: ....
[fill in your lodger's name here]
('The Lodger')

Date:

I refer to the Agreement between us by which you occupy accommodation as my lodger. The Agreement can be ended by either of us giving to the other notice of (one week/one month/three months). *[Landlord fills in according to the period set out in the Lodger Agreement.]*

By this notice to quit, I require you to vacate the accommodation on ....{date} and to leave the accommodation and the contents in the good condition which the Agreement requires.

Signed by the Landlord ....

Note: Landlord should keep a copy.

Useful contacts

Rent-a-Room details from the Inland Revenue

Call your local tax office or access
www.inlandrevenue.gov.uk

To find your local gas installer

CORGI (Council of Registered Gas Installers)
Helpline 01256 372300
www.corgi-gas.com

Free leaflets from the Office of the Deputy Prime Minister

From Citizens Advice Bureaux or www.housing.odpm.
gov.uk:

Letting Rooms in Your Home – A Guide for Resident Landlords

Your Rights as a Council Tenant – The Council Tenant's Charter

Advice on taking in lodgers, including a Lodger's Application Form

Landlordzone

www.landlordzone.co.uk

Planning permission or not?

DIY Doctor

www.diydoctor.org.uk

Definitions of a house in multiple occupation

www.housing.odpm.gov.uk/research/echs96/hmo/ann
exa

All about housing benefit

Department for Work and Pensions

www.dwp.gov.uk

Banking for landlords

Intelligent Finance

www.if.com

Smile

www.smile.co.uk

Gingerbread

www.gingerbread.org.uk

Index

Notes

Notes

Notes